THE BOSTON MASSACRE

On the night of March 5, 1770, a large crowd of local citizens surrounded British soldiers on duty in front of the Custom House in Boston, Massachusetts, baiting and threatening them. At last, the British soldiers opened fire in what they believed was self-defense. Five citizens fell, dead or mortally wounded, and a bloody battle was averted only by the prompt action of Lieutenant Governor Thomas Hutchinson. Bostonians never forgot the act of the British soldiers and never forgave them for the Boston Massacre. Years later, John Adams wrote: "On that night the foundation of American independence was laid."

PRINCIPALS

CAPTAIN THOMAS PRESTON, commander of the British soldiers on duty at the Custom House.

EIGHT BRITISH SOLDIERS, who made up the guard at the Custom House. Members of the British 29th Regiment.

LIEUTENANT GOVERNOR THOMAS HUTCHINSON, who prevented the Massacre from developing into a bloody battle.

CRISPUS ATTUCKS, a colonial ringleader in the fighting that night. He was killed instantly by British guns.

SAMUEL GRAY, a workman killed by the British guns.

JAMES CALDWELL, a mate on an American ship, killed in the fighting.

SAMUEL MAVERICK, a seventeen-year-old apprentice, mortally wounded; died on March 6.

PATRICK CARR, an artisan, mortally wounded; died on March 14.

JOHN ADAMS
JOSIAH QUINCY, JR. } Lawyers for the defense of the British soldiers at their court trial.

ROBERT TREAT PAINE
SAMUEL QUINCY } Lawyers for the colony at the court trial.

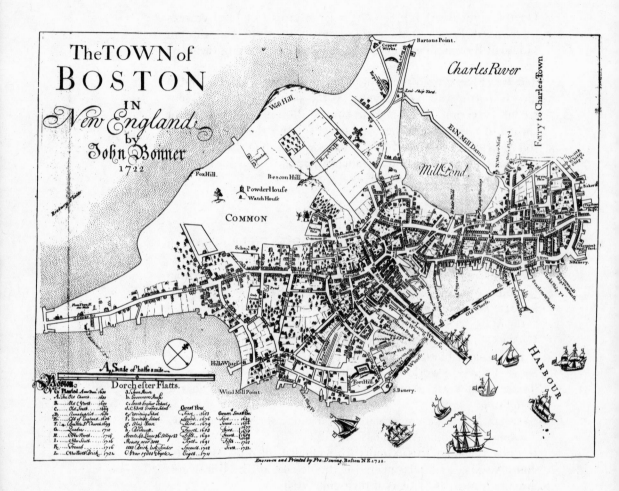

The TOWN of BOSTON IN New England by John Bonner 1722

Bartons Point.

Copper Works

Charles River

Ferry to Charles-Town

West Hill

Leis Ship Yard

E & N Mill Dam

Mill Pond.

N Watr Mill

FoxHill.

Beacon Hill

Powder House
Watch House

COMMON

School

Harbour

Old Wharfe

HARBOUR

Hill Wharf

FortHill

S. Battery.

Wind Mill Point

A Scale of half a mile.

Dorchester Flatts.

Engraven and Printed by Fra. Dewing. Boston N E 1722.

A FOCUS BOOK

The Boston Massacre

March 5, 1770

A Colonial Street Fight Erupts into Violence

by Alice Dickinson

Illustrated with contemporary prints and maps

FRANKLIN WATTS, INC.

575 Lexington Avenue   New York, N.Y. 10022

The authors and publishers of the Focus Books wish to acknowledge the helpful editorial suggestions of Professor Richard B. Morris.

Jacket photo: The Boston Massacre, by Paul Revere. (Metropolitan Museum of Art)

Contents

THE BOSTON MASSACRE

Boston Harbor and the landing of the British troops, painted by

A Night in March

It was Monday, March 5, in the year 1770. All day long, a bitter wind had whined through the gray, narrow streets of Boston, in the British colony of Massachusetts. As the citizens picked their gingerly way through the snow and ice of the footpaths they glanced uneasily at the red-coated soldiers of the British garrison stationed in the city. Trouble trembled in the air. Something unpleasant was brewing, and the British soldiers were a part of it.

Now night was falling. Overhead, a slender, silvery moon hung quiet in the sky. But Boston was astir with a strange excitement. Knots of men and boys appeared dimly in the dusk, strolling the streets carelessly, but armed with canes and sticks. In the taverns, men met to talk in guarded voices. On every corner, the low muttering of the crowd could be heard.

From Murray's barracks on Brattle Street, a dozen soldiers came out, walking nonchalantly, but armed with clubs and cutlasses. By-

Christian Remick in 1768. (Stokes Collection, New York Public Library)

standers greeted them with catcalls and whistling. For a long time, the workmen and apprentices of Boston had been quarreling with the British soldiers. The town was full of rumors that tonight the trouble might come to a head.

As the evening wore on, more gangs appeared in the streets, and fighting broke out between the soldiers and the townspeople. An English captain making his way toward Murray's barracks found his path barred by a shouting, whacking, free-for-all battle. Some of the Bostonians had been wounded by cutlasses, and there was danger that further damage might be done. Quickly the captain ordered his men into barracks, had the gate shut, and made a promise that no soldiers would be let out for the rest of the evening. At that, some of the citizens urged everyone assembled in the street to go home peaceably. But the crowd hung about, yelling insults, and daring the soldiers to come out again. The officers restrained their men with difficulty. At length, seeing that the excitement here was over, someone in the mob suggested going to the main British guardhouse on

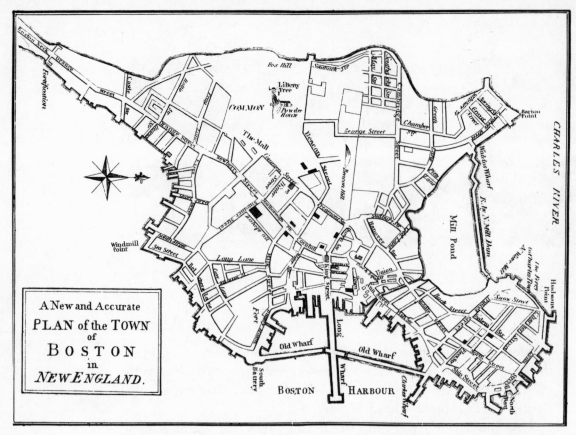

Boston in 1770. King Street runs from Long Wharf in the center of the picture. The Town House (shaded) is at the head of the street. The Custom House (shaded) is to the right and a little lower down.

King Street, in search of more soldiers.

At about this time, a boy came running through the town, crying, and complaining that the British sentry at the Custom House had hit him with the stock of his musket.

Suddenly the bell of the Old Brick Meeting House began to ring. In the frosty air and the dark, its deep, steady tolling sounded ominous and frightening.

[4]

Now more people appeared in the streets — some with buckets, for this was the bell that gave the alarm for fires. "Fire! Fire!" The words echoed through the town. But there seemed to be no fire — only the constant disturbance in the streets: the steady, threatening mutter; the muffled figures slipping through the dark, coming together for a moment, then breaking apart again.

For a few moments the town seemed fairly quiet except for the deep-toned ringing of the bell. But, about 9:15, the gang coming into King Street spied the lone sentinel standing watch in front of the hated Custom House.

"There's a soldier!"

"That's the soldier who hit the boy!"

"Knock him down! Kill him! Kill him!" The crowd was turning ugly.

Yelling and cursing and waving their sticks, the townspeople swept toward the sentinel. Alarmed, he backed up the steps of the Custom House and loaded his gun. Some of the boys in the throng circled in front of him, taunting him and pelting him with snowballs and huge chunks of ice until he cried out for help.

From the main guardhouse across the way, six British privates and a young corporal arrived on the double. They jostled their way through the crowd and halted in a half circle around the sentry box, holding their guns in front of them. The sentinel came down from the steps to join them. Almost immediately, Captain Thomas Preston, officer of the day, arrived to stand with his men.

A gang of sailors and rowdies led by a large mulatto man approached down Royal Exchange Lane, waving their weapons, large pieces of cordwood. They joined in the shouting. "Knock them down!" "Kill them!" By now, the crowd of citizens numbered fifty or sixty. Screaming and shoving and thrashing their sticks, they pressed in on the red-coated soldiers, swearing at them and challenging them to fire.

"You lobsters!" "You bloody-backs!" "Fire if you dare! Fire if you dare!"

Backed up against the Custom House, the British soldiers had no way of escaping their tormentors. They begged people to stand back, and tried to ward off the pushing, yelling crowd by pricking them with their bayonets, but it did little good. There was the sharp crack of wood on metal as the sticks of the assailants hit the British musket barrels.

A few townspeople approached to assure the soldiers that no harm would come to them, and a few tried to get the crowd to go home quietly. But things had gone too far. Suddenly, flame flashed from the British guns, and shots rang out. Five Bostonians fell, dead or mortally wounded. The crowd drew back in fright, then rushed forward again to help the injured. What had been a dangerous quarrel had in a moment flared into an ugly tragedy. For the first time, British soldiers had deliberately fired on American civilians and had killed them.

Now every bell in town was clanging wildly, and the British drums thundered in the night, beating the call to arms for the military garrison. More citizens thronged into the streets. From every direction they came running. The cry for vengeance echoed and re-echoed. "Massacre!" "Murder!" The words flashed through the crowd.

To this day, the affair is known as the Boston Massacre. Although the American Revolution was not to be fought for another five years, the colonists never forgot the Massacre or the British soldiers' part in it.

The BLOODY MASSACRE perpetrated in King—j—Street BOSTON on March 5th 1770 by a party of the 29th REGT.

BUTCHER'S HALL

Engrav'd Printed & Sold by PAUL REVERE BOSTON

Unhappy Boston! see thy Sons deplore,
Thy hallow'd Walks besmear'd with guiltless Gore.
While faithless P—n and his savage Bands,
With murd'rous Rancour stretch their bloody Hands;
Like fierce Barbarians grinning o'er their Prey,
Approve the Carnage, and enjoy the Day.

If scalding drops from Rage from Anguish Wrung,
If speechless Sorrows lab'ring for a Tongue,
Or if a weeping World can ought appease
The plaintive Ghosts of Victims such as these;
The Patriot's copious Tears for each are shed,
A glorious Tribute which embalms the Dead.

But know Fate summons to that awful Goal,
Where Justice strips the Murd'rer of his Soul:
Should venal C—ts the scandal of the Land,
Snatch the relentless Villain from her Hand,
Keen Execrations on this Plate inscrib'd,
Shall reach a Judge who never can be brib'd.

The unhappy Sufferers were Messrs Saml GRAY, Saml MAVERICK, Jams CALDWELL, CRISPUS ATTUCKS & Patk CARR
Killed. Six wounded; two of them (CHRISTr MONK & JOHN CLARK) Mortally

Paul Revere's famous print of the Boston Massacre. (Stokes Collection, New York Public Library)

From the Beginning—

In a way, events had been shaping themselves for conflict since the earliest days of settlement.

Massachusetts had been colonized by Englishmen. And Englishmen, more than any other people of their day, insisted on their rights and liberties. They valued their right to elect a representative to their government; their right to have a fair trial by jury in a court; and their right to be taxed only with the consent of their representative governing body.

More than that, the men and women who had left Britain to wrestle with the American wilderness were probably, to start with, English people with a difference. They were discontented with their lot in the homeland. They desired a newer and more abundant land, and wider freedoms than England offered. These people had perhaps a larger than usual measure of courage and energy and vision. They were willing to dare the unknown in their search for a life shaped nearer to their heart's desire.

In the new land, they found a way of living startlingly different from the one they had left behind. All around them was the wilderness, strange and forbidding, yet inviting too, challenging them daily with its hardships, its threats, and its promises. England lay far away, across the wide, tossing Atlantic — distant by a voyage of several months. In moments of crisis, what use was the king or the British government? The colonists knew only too well how much their lives depended on their own efforts.

Living at first on the edge of the forest, building their homes with their own hands, defending themselves from almost constant danger, the Englishmen of the New World could not help but change. Wilderness living made them independent and self-reliant, and prouder than ever of their liberties. They still remained English-

An old print shows early Boston settlers hard at work.

men, but they were becoming something new: American Englishmen.

As time went on, the king and Parliament seemed to matter less and less. The colonists had their local governments and laws, much like the local governments and laws they had left behind in England. But some of the English laws made no sense in the new land. And in the new land, some laws were needed that would have made no sense in England. The colonial governments began to take on an American flavor, too.

[9]

Captain John Smith's map of New England, printed in 1616. (Stokes Collection, New York Public Library)

During the earlier years of the colonies, the king and Parliament were busy with troubles at home. And always there were those three thousand miles of ocean between England and the New World. For a time, the colonists were left more or less to themselves. They flourished on the neglect, and thought it only natural that they should manage their own affairs. In fact, they came to expect this liberty.

The Colonial Governors and the Assemblies

The main governing group in each colony was the assembly, made up of men elected by the voters. The assemblies were watched over to some extent by the British government. By 1763, eight of the colonies had royal governors who represented the king. These governors received instructions from the king and were given the power to veto the laws that were passed by the assemblies. Moreover, all local laws that the governors approved were sent to England, where the king's Privy Council made the final decision on whether these laws were to be allowed.

Supporting each governor was an appointed council, which was supposed to act as a check on the elected assemblies. In many cases, the councilmen were too weak to have much effect. At times, the governors found themselves in a difficult spot, especially in some of the more high-spirited colonies. Then, if a governor carried out the king's instructions, he was bound to stir up ill will among the colonists. And if he ignored the king's instructions, he was soon in trouble at home in England.

All the while, the colonists stood firm in their belief that the assemblies should do most of the governing. There were constant skirmishes between the governor and the council on the one hand and the assemblies on the other, as the assemblies tried out their strength. When they gained the right to appropriate money and to oversee its spending, they had a mighty weapon to brandish against uncooperative governors. They could hold back the pay of officials, and they had a certain amount of choice over appointments.

Throughout the early years of the eighteenth century the assemblies continued to increase in power. Most of the laws they passed were allowed to stand, and the colonists enjoyed a great deal of political freedom.

The Navigation Acts

But the colonies had prospered and escaped invasion from other countries chiefly because English ships dominated the ocean trade routes. To maintain her strength, Britain needed the support of her whole empire. So, while the colonists may have seen themselves in one light, the British government saw them in quite another. The colonists believed that the colonies they had established were important in themselves. The British believed that the colonies were important only to help in keeping the mother country strong. From the English viewpoint, the colonists' duty was to produce raw materials that Britain could use, and to buy manufactured goods from Britain in return. This helped British industry and trade, and meant gold and silver in British banks. Nothing must be allowed to interfere with the prosperity of the empire.

But England was not the only European nation to seek colonies and trade. Rivals in the struggle for world power were France, Holland, and Spain. By 1651, Holland had managed to gain a foothold in the trade with the British American colonies. In fact, because of their fine ships and goods and easy sales terms, the Dutch were a real threat to English business not only in America but all over the trading world.

Accordingly, in 1651, and later, in 1660, 1663, 1673, and 1696, the British Parliament passed Navigation Acts aimed chiefly at encouraging English shipping and crippling the trade of rival countries. The acts provided that no goods could be imported to or exported from the colonies except in British or colonial ships, manned for the most part by sailors who were British or colonial citizens. Moreover, ships carrying products from Asia or Europe to the American colonies were expected to bring these products first to England and there to pay duties on them. After this, the goods could be shipped across the Atlantic in ships of the British Empire.

In addition, England made sure that the colonial products she needed would go to her, and to no one else without her approval. Certain colonial goods were listed, or "enumerated." These enumerated articles could be shipped from England's colonies only to Britain and Ireland. Sugar, tobacco, indigo (for making blue dye), and dyewoods were among the enumerated articles. These were the valuable products of the day, and England hoped to make her empire self-sufficient in these things.

Throughout the eighteenth century, England added more and more products to the enumerated list whenever, by so doing, she could help her own trade.

The American southern colonies fitted particularly well into Britain's plans for the empire. The crops of the South — tobacco, and later, indigo and rice — were welcomed by English merchants. In return for these products, the southern planters took British manufactured goods, at whatever prices the British merchants cared to charge. It was a fine arrangement, as far as England was concerned.

But the New England colonies were a bit of a problem to the British. Because of the thin, granite-ribbed soil and the quirky climate of the north, these colonies could not produce the agricultural goods that Britain desired. Fish and lumber were New England's greatest natural products. Except for some timber, and tall white pines for masts, Britain had no use for these products.

Seagoing New England

The New Englanders spent little time in worrying about supplying Britain with needed goods, however. Inward from the coast, New England had magnificent forests, and along the shore there were hundreds of little bays and harbors, perfect for shipbuilding. There was oak for the strong ribs of ships, and pine for masts and yardarms, and there were plenty of skilled workmen.

Some of the ships were sold to Britain. But New Englanders took naturally to the sea. Most of their ships sailed under New England sea captains — some as fishing vessels along the coasts of Maine and Nova Scotia, some as trading vessels.

The West Indies were a ready market for New England's fish and lumber. The colonists of these islands raised sugarcane, and their sugar refineries had a by-product that the New Englanders bought eagerly in return trade. This product was molasses.

Taken back to the northern distilleries, the molasses was made into rum. This liquor, in turn, became an important part of another New England venture, the African slave trade. On the coast of Guinea, Yankee traders exchanged the rum for African tribesmen, who were brought to the New World as slaves. This was a ghastly business, but a profitable one, and the traders closed their eyes to its cold-blooded cruelty.

Because the molasses of the French West Indies was much less expensive than that of the British islands, the New Englanders

A southeast view of Boston and its harbor in the 1730's. (Stokes Collection, New York Public Library)

preferred to deal with the French. In 1733, the British Parliament, spurred on by the British West Indian sugarcane growers, passed the Molasses Act, which aimed at stopping the foreign trade in this product. The act placed a heavy duty on French West Indian molasses imported into the North American colonies.

Not only did the New Englanders resent paying the duty, but they dreaded losing the French West Indian market for their fish and lumber. The British West Indies could not find a use for all the New England cargo, nor could they furnish enough molasses. New Englanders foresaw the ruin of their trade in fish and lumber and rum. At first, they stormed against the new law, then ignored it and went on buying molasses from the French islands, importing it secretly. Yankee sea captains were skilled smugglers. They knew every little inlet along their jigsaw coast, and catching them at the smuggling game was next to impossible. After a time, the British customs officers stationed in America gave up even trying seriously to enforce the molasses law.

The French and Indian War

The New Englanders' high-handed flouting of British authority, and their skill at smuggling, became a serious problem for England during the wars with France. From 1689 to 1763, there were four of these wars. But it was the last one, the French and Indian War, that concerned the American colonists the most.

This war had broken out in 1754 when France and England were both seeking control of the rich lands of the Ohio Valley. France wished to build forts and fur-trading posts in this area. These posts would connect her settlements on the Mississippi River with the rest of New France, which spread north and west of the English colonies. The British, for their part, dreaded being boxed by the French into a narrow strip of land along the coast. Already, the English colonists were moving westward a few miles at a time. The Ohio Valley offered room for British colonial growth. American traders, too, eyed the valley as a rich field for commerce with the Indians.

During the war years, the smuggling trade with the French West Indies kept up, even though the British colonial smugglers were now definitely dealing with the enemy. In one West Indian port, an observer noted one hundred ships at once, all flying the British flag and loaded with provisions for the French. In addition, traders from the northern colonies found it an easy matter to run

Louisburg in 1759. (Library of Congress)

supplies to the French troops in Louisbourg, on Cape Breton Island in New France. In return, the traders received West Indian goods, which they smuggled into their home ports.

The many provisions shipped secretly by the colonists to the enemy troops enabled the French to keep on fighting. Without the colonial provisioning, the war would almost certainly have ended sooner in French defeat.

In 1761, two years before the war ended, a dispute arose that plainly showed the difference in British and colonial thinking about the rights of the colonies and the mother country. In 1760, a British officer in the Salem, Massachusetts, customhouse had asked that a

[17]

James Otis.

general permit, called a writ of assistance, be granted him so that he might make a search for foreign goods he suspected had been smuggled into the port. Writs of this kind had been issued before. They were intended to prevent a customs officer from abusing his power, and required that he take with him an officer of the court to help him gain entry to any place where he thought smuggled goods might be stored.

The Massachusetts merchants detested search and the writs of assistance, and were against any further writs being granted. In 1761, they asked two colonial lawyers, James Otis and Oxenbridge Thacher, to plead their case against the writs in court. Thacher was quiet in his arguments, but Otis, a firebrand, made an impassioned speech that lasted four hours. He claimed that such writs were against the fundamental principles of law. The statute of Parliament that made the writs legal in the colonies was unconstitutional, Otis declared.

In the end, the writs were issued anyhow. But Otis had raised the question as to how far the British Parliament could exercise its powers in the colonies. It was a question that became more and more important as time went on.

A British Army for America

With the Treaty of 1763, peace was established between England and France. England gained the continental territory of New France east of the Mississippi River, and also acquired the territory that is now Florida, and a narrow strip of land stretching to the Mississippi. Britain had added to her empire, but she had added to her problems, too.

The taking of Quebec by the British in 1759, in the decisive battle of the French and Indian War. (Library of Congress)

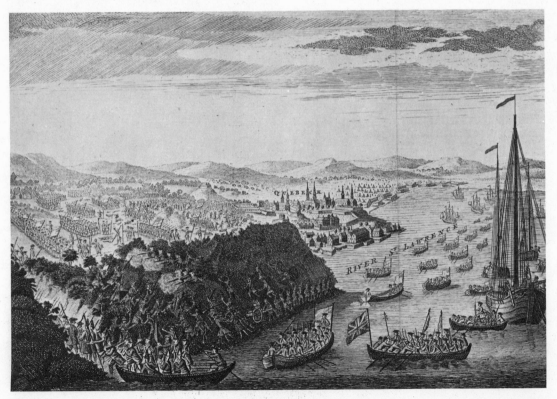

The war had been terribly expensive. To make things worse, many of the American colonies had been lukewarm about offering men and supplies to help in the fighting, and had come forward with assistance only after England had promised to repay their expenses. Now England was left with a tremendous debt.

In addition, there was another problem. The inland area of the North American continent still needed to be brought under control. The Indians, and also the French settlers, remained a possible threat to the safety of the English colonists.

In 1763, in Pontiac's War, the Indians of the Ohio Valley and the Great Lakes region rose in a massive rebellion against their trading arrangements with the British and against the entry of British colonial pioneers into what was considered Indian territory. In that same year, England, in a proclamation, pledged to honor the claims of the Indians to the lands west of the Appalachian Mountains, and pledged not to allow settlement in these areas without the natives' consent.

It seemed clear to the British that an army was needed not only to protect the English colonists but also to defend the rights of the Indians.

The English government proposed to send twenty battalions — 10,000 men — to North America, chiefly to occupy posts along the frontier and the Great Lakes and in what is now Canada. Moreover, the British thought it only fair that the colonies should help pay the cost of keeping these forces in North America. England could not afford added expenses at this time; English citizens were already staggering under a crushing load of taxes. And besides, the troops would be stationed in America for the colonists' protection.

The colonists took a jaundiced view of the British plans. The war years had been prosperous ones, the colonies were growing, and the colonists were feeling more confident and independent than ever. Now that the French had been defeated, the Americans doubted their need for protection. They were ready to expand — into the Ohio Valley, among other places.

It was unfortunate that, just at this time, England should enter the picture, seemingly intent on curtailing the colonists' freedom — by keeping them out of the Ohio Valley, by saddling them with an army they did not want, and probably by making them pay for it.

The Sugar Act

In 1763, George Grenville became England's Chancellor of the Exchequer, or its treasurer. It was his task to find a way to solve Britain's money problems, among them paying for the troops to be sent to North America. Grenville turned his attention to American smuggling, which was depriving England of much-needed customs revenue.

The customs officers plainly were not doing their duty. Many of them accepted bribes to overlook contraband goods coming in under their noses. Some of them did not even live in the colonies, but stayed comfortably at home in England, collecting their pay while deputies did their work. The whole customs system was inefficient, and the cost of keeping it running was much too high.

Now, new regulations ordered the home-staying customs officers to their posts in the colonies. They were instructed to keep exact accounts of imports and exports. As a spur to greater activity, they were offered one-half of all the ships and cargoes condemned as a result of seizure for smuggling. In addition, English warships in American waters were allowed to seize smugglers and receive rewards for so doing. Everywhere along the coast, customs officers began watching shipping more carefully. Shippers were required to fill out long forms for each cargo of goods; the whole process of law enforcement was made more favorable for the customs officers, more difficult for suspected culprits.

As it happened, the old Molasses Act of 1733 expired at this time. That act had placed a duty of sixpence a gallon on imported molasses not produced in the British West Indies. The northern importers had thought the duty too high, and few persons had even dreamed of paying it. In the new Sugar Act of 1764, this duty was lowered to threepence a gallon. But this time the British clearly intended to collect the money. In the same act, duties on some other imports were raised, and foreign rum and French wines were banned entirely as imports to the colonies.

By 1764, a postwar depression had set in. This depression, together with the Sugar Act and other commercial regulations passed by Parliament in the same year, had a deadly effect on trade and brought hard times to many parts of the colonies. The colonial importers protested the new act. And a Boston town meeting declared that it violated the rights of the colonies because it was a tax bill passed by Parliament, a governing body in which the colonies had no representatives.

The Stamp Act

Stiffening the customs procedures and collecting new duties would, after all, bring in only a small amount toward the total cost of keeping the troops in North America. Something more was needed.

A tax was possible that, to the English, seemed fair and not too burdensome to any one person. It was a stamp tax. Such a tax had long been paid by Englishmen. Now Chancellor of the Exchequer Grenville proposed that the British government place a tax, indicated by a stamp, on all colonial newspapers, legal documents, almanacs,

The so-called British stamps were impressions similar to those of a notary public today. This one indicates a tax of one shilling. (Massachusetts Historical Society)

playing cards, and numerous other articles. These stamps would vary in cost according to the use of the article on which they were placed. The money collected from the tax would go toward paying for the troops.

When the British Parliament proposed an act compelling the colonists to pay stamp taxes, a howl of protest arose from North America. Almost every business and legal transaction would require a stamp, and so would many such everyday dealings as buying a newspaper. Colonial trade was already in a slump. How in the world, the colonists demanded, could they be expected to pay this new tax when they had no money?

Their pocketbooks were the least of their worries, however. They had far greater concerns. What were the British planning? If Parliament could tax the colonies once, what was to prevent it from taxing them again and again? Eventually the assemblies might lose control of colonial finances, and the governors would no longer be

[23]

dependent on the people's will. What would happen then to the liberty that the colonists had so carefully guarded over the years?

Despite the protests and doubts of the colonies, the Stamp Act was passed by Parliament on March 22, 1765. Grenville had thought it likely that there might be some trouble in getting the colonists to accept the act. He had tried to make it as agreeable as possible to them by appointing Americans as the distributors who would actually sell the stamps. Many prominent men had accepted these appointments. They apparently had no inkling of the storm that was to arise over the Stamp Act.

It was Patrick Henry of Virginia who rallied the colonists to action. On May 29, 1765, he introduced a set of resolutions into the Virginia House of Burgesses. These resolutions stated that by their royal charters the Virginians had been granted the rights of Englishmen, and that among these rights was that of being taxed by persons they themselves had chosen to represent them. Furthermore, the resolutions stated that the Virginia assembly had the sole right and power to lay taxes on the inhabitants of Virginia, and that every attempt to vest such power in other persons would tend to destroy both British and American freedom.

When the Virginia resolutions were reprinted in the newspapers of the other colonies, two highly inflammable items had been added. These had not appeared in the resolutions as finally adopted by the House of Burgesses. The two additions stated that the Virginians were not bound to obey any taxation laws except their own, and that anyone who maintained that outside persons had the right or power to tax Virginians should be considered an enemy of the colony.

The newspaper accounts led the citizens of other colonies to believe that the Virginia House of Burgesses had decided to resist the Stamp Act. The Virginia resolutions ended the people's uncertainty. Now there was a general outcry against Parliament's right to tax the colonies. From this time on, "No taxation without representation"

Patrick Henry.

An old German print depicts the American colonists burning British stamped paper. (Library of Congress)

was the watchword. Since the colonies did not send representatives to the British Parliament, the colonists argued, that body had no right to lay taxes on them.

Even before news of the Virginia resolutions had reached the other colonies, plans were being made to resist the Stamp Act in an orderly way. In June, 1765, the Massachusetts assembly sent a letter to each of the other assemblies, suggesting that a committee from each colony meet in New York in October, to draw up a paper to be sent to King George III of England. This paper was to ask relief not only from the Stamp Act, but also from the trade acts and duties.

But in the meantime, public feeling against the Stamp Act was rising to fever heat, and some of the more fiery of the colonial newspapers were raging against the act. Real trouble broke out in Boston on August 14, 1765. There a mob of shopkeepers and workmen made an effigy of Andrew Oliver, the newly appointed stamp distributor, and hanged it, then beheaded and burned it. Not content with that, the mob wrecked Oliver's house and so intimidated him that he resigned his post the next day.

Boston soon found that it was easier to incite a mob than to calm one. On August 26, the plundering and ruination of the homes of British government officials started again. Finally, the house of Lieutenant Governor Hutchinson, an innocent victim who had nothing to do with the Stamp Act, was entered, robbed, and terribly damaged. Now, many Bostonians were aghast to see where events were leading. The colonial militia was called out, and the lawlessness was halted.

But the epidemic of mob violence had spread to other colonies. A secret organization called the Sons of Liberty had been formed. Made up chiefly of workmen and shopkeepers, the Sons of Liberty took the forefront in fighting the Stamp Act, mostly with violence. Many of their riots were apparently planned, and were sometimes led, by wealthy and prominent lawyers and merchants who were

[27]

An old British cartoon on the repeal of the Stamp Act. British ministers march in funeral procession, with Grenville bearing the coffin of the Stamp Act. Ships wait in the background to take British goods to America. (Library of Congress)

sympathetic to their aims. In colony after colony, the stamp distributors found their lives threatened and their homes wrecked. One by one, these men resigned their posts.

In October, the Stamp Act Congress addressed the king, asserting the colonists' right, as Englishmen, to be taxed only by governing bodies in which they had representatives.

November 1, 1765, was the date upon which the Stamp Act was to go into effect. After that date, according to the new law, no ship could leave port, no newspaper could be distributed, no court session

[28]

could be held, unless stamps appeared in the proper places. The Sons of Liberty saw to it that the act was not made effective. Gradually, such colonial activities as had halted on November 1 took up their normal course again, without the use of stamps.

To drive home the point more sharply, the colonists decided to put economic pressure on Britain to repeal the act. A boycott on the importation of British goods — a refusal to receive them — began in New York and spread to other colonial ports. Such a boycott inflicted heavy damage on British trade. Soon, Parliament was receiving anguished appeals from English merchants to repeal the Stamp Act.

After a long and bitter debate in both houses of Parliament, the act was finally repealed on March 18, 1766. The statute of repeal stated that continuing the act would lead to "many inconveniences," and might be harmful to British commerce. But Parliament did not back down entirely. It accompanied the repeal with a Declaratory Act stating the authority of Parliament "to make laws and statutes . . . to bind the colonies and people of America, subjects of the Crown of Great Britain, in all cases whatsoever."

The Townshend Acts

When the colonists heard of the Stamp Act's repeal, they were jubilant. Bells rang and cheers resounded.

Besides the repeal of the hated Stamp Act, Britain had taken other steps to help colonial trade. The duty on molasses was lowered from threepence to one penny a gallon, although now this rate was made to apply to British as well as to foreign-made molasses. Free ports for trading in foreign produce were also established in the West Indies.

Perhaps best of all, from the colonists' point of view, Britain had a new ministry at this time. It was headed by the colonists' favorite, William Pitt.

In the general excitement, nobody in the colonies paid much attention to the Declaratory Act and what it might mean. That was soon to be made clear.

Pitt was a sick man, plagued with gout, and too emotionally upset to carry out his duties. Much of the responsibility for solving Britain's problems fell on Charles Townshend, now Chancellor of the Exchequer. He had little patience with the colonists, and privately thought they should be given a lesson in humility.

The problem of supporting the North American troops still had not been settled, and Townshend pledged that he would find a way of raising the needed money. In due time, he proposed several laws, known altogether as the Townshend Acts. Among them were the following provisions:

1. Duties should be laid on some goods imported into the colonies: chiefly on lead, paper, paint, glass, and tea.

2. The navigation and trade acts should be more strictly enforced, and writs of assistance — general search warrants — should be issued to the customs officers in America so that they could enter buildings and ferret out hidden smuggled goods.

3. Money raised from import duties should be used not only to pay for defense in America, but also to pay court officers and royal governors in those provinces where the British might find such action necessary.

To collect the new duties, a five-man board, Commissioners of the Customs for America, was established, with headquarters in Boston. Before this time, American customs officers had received their orders from the Commissioners of Customs in London.

The Townshend Acts were passed on June 29, 1767. All portions of them were infuriating to the colonists. They saw the new duties as another form of the taxation without representation that they had resisted in the Stamp Act. They had always hated the writs of assistance as an invasion of their personal privacy. And they strongly objected to civil officers being paid by Britain rather than by the colonial assemblies. If this were to become general practice, the assemblies might soon lose all control over the governors.

Protest against the Townshend Acts was not long in coming. Again, Boston led the way. In October, 1767, a Boston town meeting, with colonial lawyer James Otis as chairman, passed a resolution calling upon the people not to use goods imported from Britain, but to manufacture articles for themselves as far as possible.

In February, 1768, the Massachusetts assembly sent a Circular Letter, drawn up by Samuel Adams, to the other assemblies. This letter denounced the Townshend Acts as being against the principle of no taxation without representation, and claimed that the proposal to pay the salaries of governors and other civil officials with Crown money was unconstitutional.

In March, 1768, Boston importers revived the idea of a non-importation agreement among Americans. Gradually, merchants in the other colonial ports joined in the movement against importing British goods.

Boston and the Customs Commissioners

While these orderly protests were going forward, the mobs were also on the move. The customs commissioners were their chief target. These gentlemen soon found that enforcing the revenue and trade acts in New England was an almost hopeless task. Smuggling was rampant, yet only a few of the lawbreaking ships had been seized. Of these, several were quickly recaptured by the colonists.

Informers against smugglers were given the tar-and-feather treatment by the colonial patriots. Bitter rioting raged along the Boston waterfront, and the customs commissioners feared for their own safety.

John Hancock, a drawing by Paul Revere for the Royal American Magazine. *(Metropolitan Museum of Art)*

The Honble JOHN HANCOCK. Esqr

When the customs officers appealed to Britain for help, the commander in chief of the Royal Navy in North America sent the fifty-gun man-of-war *Romney* to Boston, to aid in enforcing the customs laws.

Just at this time, the American sloop *Liberty* had come into harbor. The vessel was owned by John Hancock, a wealthy Boston merchant who was much in sympathy with the colonial protest group. To the customs officers, he had long been a suspected smuggler — a thorn in the flesh. On June 9, 1768, one of the customs officers claimed that Hancock had smuggled a cargo of Madeira wine into the harbor on the *Liberty* and had held the officer captive while the wine was being secretly unloaded.

With the *Romney* in port, the commissioners saw their chance to move against Hancock. The next day, they seized the *Liberty* on a legal technicality: loading without a permit — something that ships had been doing all along. While the people who were gathered on Hancock's wharf protested, the British cut the *Liberty*'s moorings and towed her out under the guns of the *Romney*.

Word of the act spread quickly, and soon a huge crowd of people had gathered. They shouted insults at the customhouse officers, then attacked them and tore their clothing. When the officers finally escaped, the crowd went on to break the windows in the houses of two of the officers, and dragged one customs collector's boat to the Common, where they burned it.

Within a day or two, the Sons of Liberty demanded that the *Romney* be ordered out of the harbor. The governor refused to go along with this request, and the patriots met to take further action. But, by this time, the customs commissioners were in such a state of nerves that they fled to Castle William, the British fort in the harbor.

Eventually, Hancock's case was tried in a vice-admiralty court, but he was not convicted of smuggling.

Castle William in Boston Harbor, where the customs commissioners took refuge. (Metropolitan Museum of Art)

British Troops Land in Boston

Even before the *Liberty* episode, Boston had been in such a condition of anarchy that the British government had instructed General Gage, commander in chief of the British forces in North America, to send one regiment or more to the town to help keep the peace and to assist the customs officers. In August, 1768, Gage ordered two regiments, the 14th and the 29th, to proceed from Halifax, Nova Scotia, to Boston.

When news reached England that the Boston mobs had chased the customs commissioners out of town, there was a terrible outcry. Boston had gone too far this time, people said. The New Englanders would have to be shown how insignificant they really were. Boston should be reduced to "a poor smuggling village." Public feeling in England ran so high that the government finally felt obliged to send two more regiments, the 64th and the 65th, from the British Isles to Boston, to aid in keeping order.

The transports carrying the Halifax troops arrived in Boston Harbor on September 29, 1768. It was a solemn day for the citizens as the men-of-war slipped silently in and took up moorings with their guns covering the town. The patriot protesters had planned to light bonfires on Beacon Hill and arouse the countryside to resist the landing of the British soldiers. But in the menacing presence of the ships the plan was dropped, and the only protests were verbal ones. The British soldiers landed without incident. As barge after barge rowed steadily in, with the troops sitting in stolid rows, uneasiness gripped the town.

On his contemporary engraving of the scene, Paul Revere, later famous for his night ride to Lexington, wrote that, upon landing, the soldiers "formed and marched with insolent pride, drums beating, fifes playing, and colors going, up King Street." The people of Boston could not overcome the feeling that their town had been occupied by the enemy.

A·VIEW·OF·PART OF·THE·TOWN·OF BOSTON·IN·NEW—

1 Beaver	5 Mermaid
2 Senegal	6 Romney
3 Martin	7 Launceston
4 Glasgow	8 Bonetta

On friday Sept.r 30th 1768. the Ships of WAR, armed Schooners, Transpor a Spring on their Cables, as for a regular Siege. At noon on Saturday t and Train of Artillery, with two peices of Cannon, landed on the Lon playing and Colours flying, up KING STREET, Each Soldier having r

Paul Revere's print of the landing of the British troops on Long Wharf in 1768. They are shown

beginning their march up King Street. (Stokes Collection, New York Public Library)

Trouble Starts

Almost at once, there were difficulties about the troops. Where were they to live? According to law, the colonies were obliged to provide quarters only after all official barracks had been filled. There were some rather dilapidated British barracks at Castle Island. But the island was several miles from the heart of the town, and troops stationed there would not be much use in an emergency. Besides, the regiments coming from Britain would eventually be quartered there.

Temporarily, the 29th Regiment camped on Boston Common, and the 14th Regiment occupied the Court House and Faneuil Hall. Cold weather was coming on, though, and the 29th needed indoor quarters. The 14th, moreover, could not stay indefinitely in public halls. Lieutenant Colonel Dalrymple, the senior officer, began to rent buildings in the town, for housing the soldiers.

James Murray, a newly arrived Scotsman, let both his own home and his large sugar house, near Dock Square. Another man rented his stores, and still another, his warehouse. Eventually, other buildings were hired throughout the town—some along the wharves, and some along a street where the city's rope makers worked.

But, with the troops so scattered, it was impossible for the officers to keep control over their men. Life in the British army in the eighteenth century was terribly hard for the men in the ranks. Pay was shockingly low; discipline was severe; the men were treated as little better than animals. It was no wonder, then, that the soldiers in Boston began deserting almost at once. Here was a new country, with open land beyond the town, and with boundless opportunities. It was easy enough to disappear. Seventy of the British soldiers deserted in their first two weeks in America.

In order to control the men, Lieutenant Colonel Dalrymple stationed guards at all the military living quarters, and placed a watch

The British troops encamped on Boston Common. A painting by Christian Remick in 1768. (Stokes Collection, New York Public Library)

around the town itself. Boston stood out in the harbor and was attached to the shore by a narrow strip of land called Boston Neck. This was a favorite escape route for the deserters. A strong guard of men was put here.

Night was the best time for deserting. Inasmuch as many of the soldiers changed into civilian clothes in order to escape detection, it became necessary for the sentries to challenge everyone who came by — citizens and soldiers alike. Bostonians bitterly resented not being able to walk about their own town without answering the cry of a British sentry, and squabbles constantly broke out between the sentries and the townspeople over this.

In the meantime, the desertion of the British soldiers kept up. In late October, General Gage arrived from his headquarters in New York. In a mood of desperation, he had a deserter executed. The citizens of Boston were shaken to see this young soldier led to the Common and shot to death. The regiments were then made to file by and view his dead body so that the lesson might be brought home more clearly.

Desertion still went on, however. In February a hard freeze set in, and even more deserters fled over the ice. When Gage ordered his troops to search the countryside for the men, local citizens refused to cooperate, and sometimes helped hide escaping soldiers. However the Americans might feel about the troops, they had no wish to send a man to the firing squad.

The British soldiers disrupted civilian life in other ways. Rum and taverns were plentiful in the town, and the soldiers had a fondness for both. Drunkenness led to street fighting, to conduct insulting to the citizens, and to small crimes such as thievery.

Then there was the matter of Sunday, a day sacred to prayer in Puritan Boston. Townspeople were horrified when the soldiers raced horses on the Common and strolled there during church hours. The commanding officers soon put a stop to both practices. In fact, the officers tried in every way possible to ease the situation that was threatening between the townspeople and the soldiers. While there was a good deal of simmering discontent that erupted now and then in a quarrel, things stayed fairly calm until the summer of 1769.

The Trouble Grows

In June of that year, a rumor spread that the 64th and 65th regiments were to be called back to Britain. The people of Boston rejoiced, and dared to hope that the other two regiments would be withdrawn also. But the British had no desire to see the customs officers driven out of town again. The 64th and 65th were allowed to go, but the 14th and 29th regiments remained.

At about this time, the mood of the Bostonians changed. They were thoroughly tired of the soldiers in their midst and they felt a sense of hopelessness about their ever departing. Now that there were fewer troops, the rowdies in the town became more daring in provoking them. One colonist even remarked that "the soldiers must now take care of themselves . . . for they are but a handful in comparison with the Sons of Liberty, who could destroy them in a moment, if they pleased."

The situation was not helped by a paper called *Journal of Events*, published by Samuel Adams and William Cooper. The *Journal* specialized in horror stories of the wrongs committed by British troops in Boston. While some of the stories were certainly true, there is no doubt that many of the accounts of the soldiers' misdeeds were pure propaganda, written to stir up ill will among the citizens. Samuel Adams, also one of the editors of the paper, was among the most radical of the leaders against the British. He had helped organize the Sons of Liberty at the time of the Stamp Act. Now he did all he could to arouse the public's feelings against the soldiers.

The street fighting and name-calling between the soldiers and the lower class of civilians became steadily worse. An increasing number of the soldiers were brought into court for various offenses. Such heavy fines were levied against them that regimental funds were soon exhausted. Then the judges bound out as indentured ser-

Samuel Adams, a drawing by Paul Revere for the Royal American Magazine. *Adams agitated unceasingly against the British soldiers. (Metropolitan Museum of Art)*

vants any soldiers who could not pay their fines.

General Gage protested, and the soldiers themselves sought vengeance in the streets. Soon neither side felt it could get justice in the courts. The soldiers were sure they would not get a fair hearing, simply because they were soldiers. Some soldier prisoners were rescued from the court by troops; others who had been accused simply disappeared. This enraged the townspeople.

Matters became worse in the autumn. On the night of October 23, 1769, trouble broke out at the guard post on Boston Neck. The ensign in charge quarreled with a citizen over supplying firewood to the post. A constable was called, and further argument took place. When a crowd gathered, the guard had to be called out to protect the post.

Next morning, during the march back to barracks, the men of the guard were badgered by angry citizens who shoved them and threw rocks at them. Finally, one workingman ran into the marching column and struck a private in the face. The private was badly cut and had to be helped along by his comrades while a sergeant fended off further attacks. The ensign kept the men from breaking ranks, and got them back to barracks without more violence, after a volley of shots had been fired into the air. But the situation had been a touchy one.

Now a sort of secret warfare set in, with civilian gangs harassing the soldiers whenever possible, and with the soldiers retaliating when they could. All winter long, a question hung in the air: When will the fighting go beyond control? The answer came on that fateful night of March 5, 1770.

Crisis

There had been one other serious cause of conflict. Military pay was so low that the British officers allowed their men to take civilian jobs, once their army duties were done for the day. The soldiers were willing to work for much lower wages than were customary. The Boston workmen, finding that jobs were continually usurped by British soldiers who would work for less money, grew more and more bitter against the army men.

The rope walks, long narrow buildings where strands of material were laid out and ropes were made for Boston's large shipping industry, were a favorite place for the soldiers to look for employment. For some time the members of the 29th Regiment had been feuding with the men who worked at the rope walks along Atkinson Street. The barracks of the 29th were in this neighborhood, and it was only natural that the soldiers should come to these rope walks for work. Neither group had any liking for the other, and they regularly quarreled and exchanged insults. The work situation only made things worse. But serious trouble did not break out until Friday, March 2, 1770. Then, one of the soldiers looking for work took offense at a particularly insulting remark made to him by a worker at Gray's rope walk. In the fight that followed, the soldier was badly beaten up.

When Thomas Walker, a big man who was a drummer for the 29th, met his comrade with blood streaming down his face, Walker and a group of the soldiers went down to the rope walk to find out what had happened. The workers were ready and waiting. Walker was carried to the hospital by his comrades.

Next, an even larger group of soldiers, armed with clubs and cutlasses, appeared at Gray's. They too were beaten back by the rope-walk men. The fighting continued on Saturday, in spite of the efforts of the owner of the rope walk to stop the trouble. On Sunday, the rope makers did not work and there was quiet. But on Monday, March 5, it was plain that the dreaded crisis was at hand. The rope makers were armed with hatchets, and gangs of civilian rowdies were beginning to assemble. The soldiers, smarting at their defeat, were jumpy and quarrelsome, and were talking loudly of vengeance. A British sergeant was missing, and his commanding officer could not help but wonder if he had been murdered.

Throughout the day, word spread that the moment of reckoning had arrived. The warring groups were ready. The final events

Paul Revere, silversmith and artist, whose on-the-spot drawings of pre-Revolutionary times are valuable to historians today. A portrait by John Singleton Copley. (Boston Museum of Fine Arts)

had been set in motion. They led that night to the tragic shooting of the five Americans by the British guard stationed in front of the Custom House. It was the so-called Boston Massacre.

The Victims of the Massacre

One of the victims of the Massacre was Crispus Attucks, probably a mulatto, part Indian or part Negro. He was born in Framingham, Massachusetts, and had been a slave. Twenty years before, he had run away from his master, and a Boston newspaper had carried an advertisement asking for help in finding him. At the time of the Massacre he was evidently on his way to North Carolina. He may have been a sailor. A big man, over six feet tall, he seems to have appointed himself a leader in the rioting. He had been seen earlier in the evening, fighting at the head of a group of sailors all armed with stout bludgeons of cordwood. When the soldiers at the Custom House were desperately trying to make their attackers stand back, he had appeared again with his group, cursing and threatening, and daring the soldiers to shoot. He had been in the forefront of the rioters and was instantly killed when the guns sounded.

Samuel Gray, another of those instantly killed, had been a worker at the rope walk where the fighting had started on March 2. He had evidently taken part in the rioting before the Custom House, and was shot as he stood with both hands at his chest.

James Caldwell, a mate on an American ship, also died at once. He apparently had not been in the fighting, but had heard the bells and the noise and had come out of his house to see what was happening.

Samuel Maverick, another victim, was a promising young man of seventeen — an apprentice to an ivory cutter. He had run from his home upon hearing the commotion, and was caught in the line of fire. He died on the morning of March 6.

Patrick Carr was mortally wounded, but did not die until March 14. A leather-breeches maker, he appears to have been an exceptionally fair-minded man. At various times before his death he talked to his doctor about the affair. He had come from Ireland, he said, and had witnessed many riots there, but none as bad as the one that had set the stage for the Massacre. He had never seen soldiers take so much abuse so patiently, and he said in all honesty that he did not blame the man who shot him. The soldiers, as Carr saw it, were threatened, and had acted in self-defense.

A Battle Is Averted

But, whoever was to blame, shots had been fired, five men had been killed or mortally wounded, and Boston was in an uproar. After the first volley of shots that evening, the soldiers had reloaded and had been about to fire again when Captain Preston dashed in front of them, striking up their musket barrels and commanding them not to shoot. He then, with some difficulty, withdrew the men across the street to the protection of the main guardhouse.

In the meantime, the rolling of the drums had called out several companies of the 29th Regiment. They were quickly formed into three divisions before the guardhouse, with the front division in a kneeling position, for firing if necessary. The 14th Regiment was ordered under arms, but remained in barracks. The situation was tense. The crowd and the confusion were growing, and people were crying out to each other, "To arms! Get out your arms!" In King Street, the civilians and the armed soldiers stood facing each other.

Lieutenant Governor Hutchinson, at his home, had heard the bells and had thought them a fire alarm. But, at a little before ten o'clock, one of the Bostonians came running and begged him to come to King Street at once. Unless something were done, Hutchinson was warned, the whole town would soon be engaged in a bloody battle.

[47]

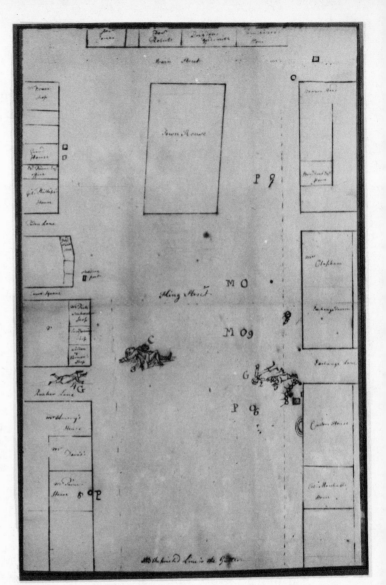

Paul Revere's sketched plan of the Boston Massacre. The British soldiers are seen in a group at the lower right. (Boston Public Library)

He started out immediately, but found himself in the midst of a huge crowd armed with clubs and swords, and all calling for firearms. Slipping through a dwelling house, he took a private way and arrived at King Street.

Immediately he questioned Captain Preston and reprimanded him for allowing the men to fire, saying that the captain had no authority to order this action.

"I was obliged to, to save the sentry," was Preston's reply.

But the crowd was growing impatient. "To the Town House," they shouted.

Hutchinson was forced into this central government building, which stood nearby. A few minutes later, he appeared on the balcony. From here, he spoke to the people, promising them that "the law should have its course," and that in the morning there would be an inquiry into the whole affair. But this promise did not satisfy the crowd. Upon their insistence, Captain Preston was arrested and the questioning of him started at once.

The people also asked that Hutchinson get the troops out of the street and into barracks. Lieutenant Colonel Dalrymple was called. When he returned to his men, they were ordered to shoulder arms and were marched into barracks. Only then did the sullen crowd begin slowly to dwindle away.

Three hours later, Captain Preston, after his questioning, was held for trial. Later still, the eight soldiers who were said to have fired on the crowd were arrested. It was three o'clock in the morning before Hutchinson finally left the Town House. His dignified and level-headed handling of the situation had spared Boston further bloodshed.

The next day, Hutchinson and Dalrymple reluctantly agreed to the demands of the citizens and withdrew the troops from the town to Castle Island. This action prevented more trouble.

Three days later, while bells tolled mournfully, the four victims of the Massacre who had then died were taken to their one grave in the Old Granary Burial Ground. Shops closed, and the inhabitants of the town assembled, and marched six abreast accompanying the coffins and followed by the carriages of the gentry.

B O S T O N, March 12.

THE Town of Boston affords a recent and melancholy Demonstration of the destructive Consequences of quartering Troops among Citizens in a Time of Peace, under a Pretence of supporting the Laws and aiding Civil Authority; every considerate and unprejudic'd Person among us was deeply impress'd with the Apprehension of these Consequences when it was known that a Number of Regiments were ordered to this Town under such a Pretext, but in Reality to inforce oppressive Measures; to awe & controul the legislative as well as executive Power of the Province, and to quell a Spirit of Liberty, which however it may have been basely oppos'd and even ridicul'd by some, would do Honor to any Age or Country. A few Persons amongst us had determin'd to use all their Influence to procure so destructive a Measure with a View to their securely enjoying the Profits of an American Revenue, and unhappily both for Britain and this Country they found Means to effect it.

It is to Governor Bernard, the Commissioners, their Confidents and Coadjutors, that we are indebted as the procuring Cause of a military Power in this Capital—The Boston Journal of Occurrences, as printed in Mr. Holt's York Gazette, from Time to Time, afforded many striking Instances of the Distresses brought upon the Inhabitants by this Measure; and since those Journals have been discontinued, our Troubles from that Quarter have been growing upon us: We have known a Party of Soldiers in the face of Day fire off a loaden Musket upon the Inhabitants, others have been prick'd with Bayonets, and even our Magistrates assaulted and put in Danger of their Lives, when Offenders brought before them have been rescued; and why those and other bold and base Criminals have as yet escaped the Punishment due to their Crimes, may be soon Matter of Enquiry by the Representative Body of this People—It is natural to suppose that when the Inhabitants of this Town saw those Laws which had been enacted for their Security, and which they were ambitious of holding up to the Soldiery, eluded, they should more commonly resent for themselves—and accordingly it has so happened; many have been the Squabbles between them and the Soldiery; but it seems their being often worsted by our Youth in those Rencounters, has only serv'd to irritate the former—What passed at Mr. Gray's Rope-walk, has already been given the Public, & may be said to have led the Way to the late Catastrophe—That the Rope-walk Lads when attacked by superior Numbers should defend themselves with so much Spirit and Success in the Club-way, was too mortifying, and perhaps it may hereafter appear, that even some of their Officers were *unhappily* affected with this Circumstance: Divers Stories were propagated among the Soldiery, that serv'd to agitate their Spirits; particularly on the Sabbath, that one Chambers, a Sergeant, represented as a sober Man, had been missing the preceeding Day, and must therefore have been murdered by the Townsmen; an Officer of Distinction so far credited this Report, that he enter'd Mr. Gray's Rope-walk that Sabbath; and when required of by that Gentleman as soon as he could meet him, the Occasion of his so doing, the Officer reply'd, that it was to look if the Serjeant said to be murdered had not been hid there; this sober Serjeant was found on the Monday unhurt, in a House of Pleasure—The Evidences already collected shew, that many Threatnings had been thrown out by the Soldiery, but we do not pretend to say that there was any preconcerted Plan, when the Evidences are published, the World will judge—We may however venture to declare, that it appears too probable from their Conduct, that some of the Soldiery aimed to draw and provoke the Townsmen into Squabbles, and that they then intended to make Use of other Weapons than Canes, Clubs or Bludgeons.

Our Readers will doubtless expect a circumstantial Account of the tragical Affair on Monday Night last; but we hope they will excuse our being so particular as we should have been, had we not seen that the Town was intending an Enquiry & full Representation thereof.

On the Evening of Monday, being the 5th Current, several Soldiers of the 29th Regiment were seen parading the Streets with their drawn Cutlasses and Bayonets, abusing and wounding Numbers of the Inhabitants.

A few minutes after nine o'clock, four youths, named Edward Archbald, William Merchant, Francis Archbald, and John Leech, jun. came ... Cornhill together, and seperating at Doctor ... corner, the two former were pa... ...lley leading to Murray's ba... ...ier brandishing a b... ...inst the ...

...ter part of the combat, and when the boys had dispersed he met the ten or 12 soldiers aforesaid rushing down the alley towards the square, and asked them if they intended to murder people? They answered Yes, by G—d, root and branch! With that one of them struck Mr. Atwood with a club, which was repeated by another, and being unarmed he turned to go off, and received a wound on the left shoulder which reached the bone and gave him much pain. Retreating a few steps, Mr. Atwood met two officers and said, Gentlemen, what is the matter? They answered, you'll see by and by. Immediately after, those heroes appeared in the square, asking where were the boogers? where were the cowards? But notwithstanding their fierceness to naked men, one of them advanced towards a youth who had a split of a raw stave in his hand, and said damn them here is one of them; but the young man seeing a person near him with a drawn sword and good cane ready to support him, held up his stave in defiance, and they quietly passed by him up the little alley by Mr. Silsby's to Kingstreet, where they attacked single and unarmed persons till they raised much clamor, and then turned down Cornhill street, insulting all they met in like manner, and pursuing some to their very doors. Thirty or forty persons, mostly lads, being by this means gathered in Kingstreet, Capt. Preston, with a party of men with charged bayonets, came from the main guard to the Commissioners house, the soldiers pushing their bayonets, crying, Make way! They took place by the custom-house, and continuing to push to drive the people off, pricked some in several places; on which they were clamorous, and, it is said, threw snow-balls. On this, the Captain commanded them to fire, and more snow-balls coming, he again said, Damn you, Fire, be the consequence what it will! One soldier then fired, and a townsman with a cudgel struck him over the hands with such force that he dropt his firelock; and rushing forward aimed a blow at the Captain's head, which graz'd his hat and fell pretty heavy upon his arm: However, the soldiers continued the fire, successively, till 7 or 8, or as some say 11 guns were discharged.

By this fatal manœuvre, three men were laid dead on the spot, and two more struggling for life; but what shewed a degree of cruelty unknown to British troops, at least since the house of Hanover has directed their operations, was an attempt to fire upon or push with their bayonets the persons who undertook to remove the slain and wounded!

Mr. Benjamin Leigh, now undertaker in the Delph Manufactory, came up, and after some conversation with Capt. Preston, relative to his conduct in this affair, advised him to draw off his men, with which he complied.

The dead are Mr. Samuel Gray, killed on the spot, the ball entering his head and beating off a large portion of his skull.

A mulatto man, named Crispus Attucks, who was born in Framingham, but lately belonged to New-Providence and was here in order to go for North-Carolina, also killed instantly; two balls entering his breast, one of them in special goring the right lobe of the lungs, and a great part of the liver most horribly.

Mr. James Caldwell, mate of Capt. Morton's vessel, in like manner killed by two balls entering his back.

Mr. Samuel Maverick, a promising youth of 17 years of age, son of the widow Maverick, and an apprentice to Mr. Greenwood, Ivory-Turner, mortally wounded, a ball went through his belly ... cut out at his back: He died the nex... ...d named Christopher M...

...great Numbers soon assembled at the Place where this tragical Scene had been acted; their Feelings may be better conceived than express'd; and while some were taking Care of the Dead and Wounded, the Rest were in Consultation what to do in those dreadful Circumstances.—But so little intimidated were they, notwithstanding their being within a few Yards of the Main-Guard, and seeing the 29th Regiment under Arms, and drawn up in King-Street; that they kept their Station and appear'd as an Officer of Rank express'd it, ready to run upon the very Muzzles of their Muskets.—The Lieut. Governor soon came into the Town-House, and there met some of his Majesty's Council, and a Number of Civil Magistrates; a considerable Body of the People immediately entered the Council Chamber, and expressed themselves to his Honor with a Freedom and Warmth becoming the occasion. He used his utmost Endeavours to pacify them, requesting that they would let the Matter subside for the Night, and promising to do all in his Power that Justice should be done, and the Law have its Course; Men of Influence and Weight with the People were not wanting on their part to procure their Compliance with his Hono'rs Request, by representing the horrible Consequences of a promiscuous and rash Engagement in the Night, and assuring them that such Measures should be entered upon in the Morning, as would be agreeable to their Dignity, and a more likely way of obtaining the best Satisfaction for the Blood of their Fellow-Townsmen.—The Inhabitants attended to these Suggestions, and the Regiment under Arms being ordered to their Barracks, which was insisted upon by the People, they then separated & returned to their Dwellings by One o'Clock. At 3 o'Clock Capt. Preston was committed, as were the Soldiers who fir'd, a few Hours after him.

Tuesday Morning presented a most shocking Scene, the Blood of our Fellow Citizens running like Water thro' King-Street, and the Merchants Exchange the principal Spot of the Military Parade for about 18 Months past. Our Blood might also be track'd up to the Head of Long-Lane, and through divers other Streets and Passages.

At eleven o'clock the inhabitants met at Faneuil-Hall, and after some animated speeches becoming the occasion, they chose a Committee of 15 respectable Gentlemen to wait upon the Lieut. Governor in Council, to request of him to issue his Orders for the immediate removal of the troops.

The Message was in these Words:

THAT it is the unanimous opinion of this meeting that the inhabitants and soldiery can no longer live together in safety; that nothing can rationally be expected to restore the peace of the town & prevent further blood & carnage, but the immediate removal of the Troops; and that we therefore most fervently pray his Honor that his power and influence may be exerted for their instant removal.

His Honor's Reply, which was laid before the Town then Adjourn'd to the Old South Meeting-House, was as follows,

Gentlemen,

I AM extremely sorry for the unhappy differences between the inhabitants and troops, and especially for the action of the last evening, and I have exerted myself upon that occasion that a due enquiry may be made, and that the law may have its course. I have in council consulted with the commanding officers of the two regiments who are in the town. They have their orders from the General at New-York. It is not in my power to countermand those orders. The Council have desired that the two regiments may be removed to the Castle. From the particular concern which the 29th regiment has had in your differences, Col. Dalrymple who is the commanding officer of the troops has signified that that regiment shall without delay be placed in the barracks at the Castle until he can send to the General and receive his further orders concerning both the regiments, and that the main guard shall be removed, and the 14th regiment so disposed and laid under such restraint that all occasion of future disturbances may be prevented.

The foregoing Reply having been read and fully considered—the question was put, Whether the Report be satisfactory? Passed in the Negative, (only 1 dissentient.) out of upwards of 4000 Voters.

It was then moved and voted John Hancock, Esq; Mr. Samuel Adam... Mr. William Molineux, William Phillips, Es... ...Warren, Joshua Henshaw, Esq; and S... ... Committee to wait on his ... ...form him, that it is ...

The 29th Regiment have already left us, and the 14th Regiment are following them, so that we expect the Town will soon be clear of all the Troops. The Wisdom and true Policy of his Majesty's Council and Col. Dalrymple the Commander appear in this Measure. Two Regiments in the midst of this populous City; and the Inhabitants justly incensed: Those of the neighbouring Towns actually under Arms upon the first Report of the Massacre, and the Signal only wanting to bring in a few Hours to the Gates of this City many Thousands of our brave Brethren in the Country, deeply affected with our Distresses, and to whom we are greatly obliged on this Occasion—No one knows where this would have ended, and what important Consequences even to the whole British Empire might have followed, which our Moderation & Loyalty upon so trying an Occasion, and our Faith in the Commander's Assurances have happily prevented.

Last Thursday, agreeable to a general Request of the Inhabitants, and by the Consent of Parents and Friends, were carried to their Grave in Succession, the Bodies of *Samuel Gray, Samuel Maverick, James Caldwell,* and *Crispus Attucks,* the unhappy Victims who fell in the bloody Massacre of the Monday Evening preceeding!

On this Occasion most of the Shops in Town were shut, all the Bells were ordered to toll a solemn Peal, as were also those in the neighboring Towns of Charlestown Roxbury, &c. The Procession began to move between the Hours of 4 and 5 in the Afternoon; two of the unfortunate Sufferers, viz. Mess. *James Caldwell* and *Crispus Attucks,* who were Strangers, borne from Faneuil-Hall, attended by a numerous Train of Persons of all Ranks; and the other two, viz. Mr. *Samuel Gray,* from the House of Mr. Benjamin Gray, (his Brother) on the North-side the Exchange, and Mr. *Maverick,* from the House of his distressed Mother Mrs. *Mary Maverick,* in Union-Street, each followed by their respective Relations and Friends: The several Hearses forming a Junction in King-Street, the Theatre of that inhuman Tragedy! proceeded from thence thro' the Main-Street, lengthened by an immense Concourse of People, so numerous as to be obliged to follow in Ranks of six, and brought up by a long Train of Carriages belonging to the principal Gentry of the Town. The Bodies were deposited in one Vault in the middle Burying-ground: The aggravated Circumstances of their Death, the Distress and Sorrow visible in every Countenance, together with the peculiar Solemnity with which the whole Funeral was conducted, surpass Description.

A military watch has been kept every night at the town-house and prison, in which many of the most respectable gentlemen of the town have appeared as the common soldier, and night after night have given their attendance.

A Servant Boy of one Manwaring the Tide-waiter from Quebec is now in Goal, having deposed that himself, by the Order and Encouragement of his Superiors had discharged a Musket several Times from one of the Windows of the House in King-Street, hired by the Commissioners and Custom House Officers to do their Business in; more than one other Person swore upon Oath, that they apprehended several Discharges came from that Quarter.—It is not improbable that we may soon be able to account for the Assassination of Mr. Otis some Time past; the Message by Wilmot, who came from the same House to the infamous Richardson before his firing the Gun which kill'd young Snider, and to open up such a Scene of Villainy acted by a dirty Banditti, as must astonish the Public.

It is supposed that there must have been a greater Number of People from Town and Country at the Funeral *those who were massacred by the Soldiers, than were* ...ter on this Continent on any Occasion.

...dreadful Tragedy has been acted by
...Boston. New-England, that...

A part of the account of the Massacre from the Boston Gazette, *March 12, 1770.* The four coffins drawn by Paul Revere bear the initials of Samuel Gray, Samuel Maverick, James Caldwell, and Crispus Attucks. At that time, Patrick Carr was still alive. (*Massachusetts Historical Society*)

John Adams, one of the lawyers for the British soldiers at their trial.

The Trial of the Soldiers

The most fiery of the citizens demanded an immediate trial of the soldiers, but Hutchinson succeeded in having it postponed until fall. When it took place, two outstanding Boston lawyers, John Adams and Josiah Quincy, Jr., defended the army men.

Later, John Adams, who was to become the second President of the United States, wrote of how he became a lawyer for the British soldiers.

'On the morning after the Massacre he had been sitting in his office near the Town House when a Mr. Forrest, a friend of Captain Preston's, came in. Tears streamed down Forrest's face as he told of Preston. He was in prison and could not get a lawyer to defend him. Forrest had been to Josiah Quincy, who had said he would take the case, but only if John Adams would help him.

"I had no hesitation in answering that counsel ought to be the very last thing that an accused person should want in a free country," wrote Adams, "that the bar [lawyers] ought to be independent and impartial at all times, and in every circumstance, and that persons whose lives were at stake ought to have the counsel they preferred." He warned Forrest, however, that this would be as important a case as had ever been tried in any court or country of the world, and that Preston must not expect Adams to rely on anything but the true evidence and the law.

Forrest had replied that Captain Preston asked no more than this and that he would gladly entrust his life to John Adams on these terms.

"If he thinks he cannot have a fair trial without my assistance, without hesitation he shall have it," Adams had answered. Besides defending Preston, Josiah Quincy and John Adams defended the other soldiers as well.

The trial of the eight soldiers began on November 27, 1770. The lawyers for the colony and the citizens were Robert Treat Paine and Samuel Quincy. After a jury of twelve men had been chosen, the pleading of the case began. The eight British soldiers of the guard stood accused of murder.

The lawyers for the colony demanded that they be allowed to show how menacing the conduct of the soldiers had been to the townspeople for a long time before the Massacre. The lawyers for the soldiers agreed, provided that they might do the same with respect to the townspeople.

[53]

The lawyers for the colony spoke as follows: "The soldiers marched through the town with all the ensigns of triumph! and evidently designed to subject the inhabitants to the severe discipline of a garrison! They have been continuing their enormities by abusing the people, rescuing prisoners out of the hands of justice, and even firing on inhabitants in the street.

"On Friday 2nd, a quarrel arose between some soldiers of the 29th and the rope-walker's journeymen and apprentices, which was carried to that length as to become dangerous to the lives of each party, many of them being much wounded. . . .

"Besides this, there was challenging of the inhabitants by sentinels posted in all parts of the town . . . which occasioned many quarrels and uneasiness. . . .

"The attack of soldiers on some of the magistrates of the town, the repeated rescues of soldiers from peace officers, the firing of a loaded musket in a public street, to the endangering of a great number of peaceable inhabitants, the frequent wounding by their bayonets and cutlasses, and numerous instances of bad behavior in the soldiery made us early sensible that troops were not sent here for the benefit of the town, and that we had no good to expect from such conservators of the peace."

In reply, John Adams spoke for the soldiers. He was well aware that there had been a definite plot by the Bostonian protesters to force the removal of the soldiers. As he later wrote: "Endeavors had been systematically pursued for many months by certain busy characters to excite quarrels, encounters, and combats, single or compound, in the night, between inhabitants of the lower class and the soldiers and at all risks to kindle immortal hatred between them."

In court, ample evidence was given to show that there had been a carefully designed plan among some of the townspeople to drive the soldiers out. Adams did not allow this testimony to be developed too far, but put a stop to it — perhaps because he feared that criti-

[54]

Samuel Quincy, one of the lawyers for the colonists at the trial. Portrait by John Singleton Copley. (Boston Museum of Fine Arts)

cism of their town would arouse the jury's antagonism too much, or perhaps because, though he was defending the soldiers staunchly and well, he still sympathized with his fellow townsmen and wanted to keep their friendship. He decided to win the case on other grounds.

The citizens had been provoked to rioting, Samuel Quincy and

Paine contended. There had been no occasion for the soldiers' firing; this had been a deliberate action. Various witnesses testified that they had heard the soldiers threaten to fire if the townspeople did not stand back, and that one of the soldiers had previously said he would be happy to shoot any of the Bostonians who annoyed him.

Several witnesses swore that they had heard Captain Preston give the command to fire. With the bells making such a din, with some people shouting "Where is the fire?" and with others screaming at the soldiers, "Fire if you dare!" this point could not be proved. It was never made clear who, if anyone, had given the order to fire. To the day of his death, years later, Preston denied that it was he.

Other witnesses testified that there had been firing from the Custom House itself. This point also was never proved.

John Adams and Josiah Quincy brought out testimony for the defense of the soldiers.

One man, James Thompson, gave testimony that hinted at a premeditated plan on the part of the townspeople. "At nine o'clock," he said, "I passed up through King Street. No person was there; the sentry was alone in Green's Lane. I and another person met about fifteen persons, with sticks in their hands. As they passed us, I heard some of them say, 'We are rather too soon.' I went on board a vessel at Griffin's Wharf and said to the people, 'I am afraid there will be mischief tonight, for I met a number of people and they seemed to hint they were about something.' Soon the bells rang. . . . I heard a woman say at a distance, 'It is no fire. Good God! there will be murder committed this night.' "

Patrick Keaton, a Bostonian, gave evidence of his experiences that night. "On the evening of the 5th of March, I was at my lodgings. I heard a noise and went out towards Union Street, and saw people coming from the North End with sticks and clubs in their hands; it was about nine o'clock. I followed them to Dock Square. Somebody asked what was the matter. He was answered that a boy and a soldier had been afoul of one another. They hallooed, 'King Street.' I went up to the foot of Jenkins' Lane, and there I saw a tall mulatto fellow, the same that was killed. He had two clubs in his hand, and he said, 'Here, take one of them.' I did so."

Q. (Lawyer's question.) "What sort of clubs were they?"

A. (Witness's answer.) "They were cordwood sticks; I went up to the head of the lane, and I dropped the stick in the snow; he went on cursing and swearing at the soldiers, down towards where the people surrounded the soldiers. I stood by the stone steps of the Custom House. There were people coming from all parts, calling out, 'Bloody-back!' and one thing and another. I could not distinguish what one-half of them said."

The testimony of witnesses was often conflicting. The lawyers of both sides did establish that a large crowd had threatened the soldiers, had thrown missiles at them — ice, sticks, oyster shells, and snowballs — and had pressed in so near to the soldiers that they had touched the muzzles of their guns.

Here is testimony from one witness.

Q. (Lawyer's question.) "Was anything thrown at the soldiers?"

A. (Witness's answer.) "Yes, there were many things thrown; what they were I cannot say."

Q. "How did the soldiers stand?"

A. "They stood with their pieces before them to defend themselves, and as soon as they had placed themselves, a party, about twelve in number, with sticks in their hands, who stood in the middle of the street, gave three cheers, and immediately surrounded the soldiers, and struck upon their guns with their sticks, and passed along the front of the soldiers, towards Royal Exchange Lane, striking the soldiers' guns as they passed; numbers were continually coming down the street."

Q. "Did you hear any bell ring?"

A. "Yes."

Q. "What bell?"

A. "I believe all the bells in town were ringing. I heard the Old South first."

Q. "Did the clattering of blows on the guns to the right, immediately before the first gun went off, appear very violent?"

A. "Yes, very violent."

Several witnesses testified that one of the soldiers had been knocked down in the struggle. The soldiers had threatened to shoot if pressed too hard. There was some confusion as to where each of them had stood, and as to which ones had fired the fatal shots.

Repeatedly the soldiers had begged the citizens to step back and had stated that they were on duty and should be left alone. Several witnesses also said that the ringing of the first bell and the alarm cry of "Fire!" had been prearranged, in order to start the other bells ringing and to call the citizens into the streets, presumably to help in fire fighting, but actually to help in the rioting.

The lawyers for the soldiers argued that the military watch had been lawfully assembled, in the course of duty, while the citizens had been most unlawfully assembled and had been bent on mischief.

John Adams and Josiah Quincy also pleaded that the soldiers had acted in self-defense, while the citizens had no other reason for their acts but vengeance for the misdeeds of the soldiers in general — not of these soldiers in particular.

Said John Adams: "Put yourself in the place of Wemms and Killroy [two of the soldiers]. Many of the people who were there were thoughtless and inconsiderate. . . . They, the soldiers, had no friends about them; with all the bells ringing to call the town together to assist the people in King Street; for they knew by that time that there was no fire; the people shouting, huzzaing and making the mob whistle; the people crying 'Kill them! Kill them! Knock them down!' heaving snowballs, oyster shells, clubs, white birch

[58]

sticks three and one-half inches in diameter. Consider this, and think whether a reasonable man in the soldier's situation would not have concluded they were going to kill him." The soldiers had no other recourse but to fire, the defense argued.

Josiah Quincy reminded the jury that the soldiers were citizens too, and had the same rights to justice as others.

The soldiers were being blamed for certain things over which they had no control, he said. "A general opinion is almost universal throughout this continent that their [the Americans'] liberties have been invaded. It is believed that the soldiers came here to enforce these acts. Mankind act from feeling more than reasoning." The object of resentment [the British Parliament] was out of reach, Quincy said, so the colonists' ill will had fallen on the British soldiers, who were only innocent instruments for carrying out the acts of government.

The soldiers' cause had attracted the attention of the whole continent if not all of Europe, Josiah Quincy warned the jury. "You ought to be careful to give a verdict that will bear the examination of time, when the pulse which now beats will beat no more. Do nothing which will hereafter bite like a serpent and sting like an adder. These persons were upon their duty and their lives were in danger if they moved from their station."

Captain Preston had already been found not guilty in an earlier trial. When the jury brought in the verdict on his men, six of them were found not guilty. The other two men were found guilty of manslaughter. These two soldiers were allowed to plead their "benefit of clergy." Benefit of clergy was a practice, in those days, carried over from medieval times, in which a clergyman could not be punished by a secular court if he could prove his status, but would be turned over to a church court for a possibly more lenient sentence. The usual sign of a clergyman had been the ability to read. In time, anyone who could read could claim benefit of clergy in some cases.

A MONUMENTAL INSCRIPTION

ON THE

Fifth of March.

Together with a few LINES

On the Enlargement of

EBENEZER RICHARDSON,

Convicted of MURDER.

AMERICANS!
BEAR IN REMEMBRANCE
The HORRID MASSACRE!
Perpetrated in King-ftreet, BOSTON,
New-England,
On the Evening of March the Fifth, 1770.
When FIVE of your fellow countrymen,
GRAY, MAVERICK, CALDWELL, ATTUCKS,
and CARR,
Lay wallowing in their Gore!
Being *bafely*, and moft *inhumanly*
MURDERED!
And SIX others badly WOUNDED!
By a Party of the XXIXth Regiment,
Under the command of Capt. Tho. Prefton.
REMEMBER!
That Two of the Murderers
Were convicted of MANSLAUGHTER!
By a Jury, of whom I fhall fay
NOTHING,
Branded in the hand!
And *difmiffed*,
The others were ACQUITTED,
And their Captain PENSIONED!
Alfo,

BEAR IN REMEMBRANCE
That on the 22d Day of February, 1770.
The infamous
EBENEZER RICHARDSON, Informer,
And tool to Minifterial hirelings,
Moft *barbaroufly*
MURDERED
CHRISTOPHER SEIDER,
An innocent youth!
Of which crime he was found guilty
By his Country
On Friday April 20th, 1770;
But remained *Unfentenced*
On Saturday the 22d Day of February, 1772.
When the GRAND INQUEST
For Suffolk county,
Were informed, at requeft,
By the Judges of the Superior Court,
That EBENEZER RICHARDSON'S *Cafe*
Then lay before bis MAJESTY.
Therefore faid *Richardfon*
This day, MARCH FIFTH! 1772.
Remains UNHANGED!!!
Let THESE things be told to Pofterity!
And handed down
From Generation to Generation,
'Till Time fhall be no more!
Forever may AMERICA be preferved,
From weak and wicked monarchs,
Tyrannical Minifters,
Abandoned Governors,
Their Underlings and Hirelings!
And may the
Machinations of artful, *defigning* wretches,
Who would ENSLAVE THIS People,
Come to an end,
Let their NAMES and MEMORIES
Be buried in eternal oblivion,
And the PRESS,
For a *SCOURGE* to Tyrannical Rulers,
Remain FREE.

AWAKE my drowfy Thoughts ! Awake my mufe!
Awake O earth, and tremble at the news !
In grand defiance to the laws of God,
The Guilty, Guilty murd'rer walks abroad,
That city mourns, (the cry comes from the ground,)
Where law and juftice never can be found :
Oh ! fword of vengeance, fall thou on the race
Of thofe who hinder juftice from its place.
O MURD'RER ! RICHARDSON ! with their lateft breath
Millions will curfe you when you fleep in death !
Infernal horrors fure will fhake your foul
When o'er your head the awful thunders roll.
Earth cannot hide you, always will the cry
Of Murder ! Murder ! haunt you 'till you die !
To yonder grave ! with trembling joints repair,
Remember, SEIDER'S corps lies mould'ring there ;
There drop a tear, and think what you have done !
Then judge how you can live beneath the Sun.
A PARDON may arrive ! You laws defy,
But Heaven's laws will ftand when KINGS fhall die.
Oh ! Wretched man ! the monfter of the times,
You were not hung " by reafon of *old* Lines,"
Old Lines thrown by, 'twas then we were in hopes,
That you would foon be hung with *new màde* Ropes ✳
But neither *Ropes nor Lines*, will fatisfiy
For SEIDER'S blood ! But GOD is ever nigh,
And guilty fouls will not unpunifh'd go
Tho' they're excus'd by judges here below !
You are enlarg'd but curfed is your fate
Tho' ⸸Cufhing's eas'd you from the prifon gate
The ✳Bridge of *Tories*, it has borne you o'er
Yet you e'er long may meet with HELL's dark fhore.

"Lins"- the name of one of the judges
✳ Name of another judge newly annamed
⸸ Do: of another of the judges
✳ Trowbridge another judge:

The two soldiers met the condition for benefit of clergy and were let off after their left thumbs had been branded in an open court by burning. (This mark was made to show that they had already pleaded benefit of clergy the one time the law allowed.)

Aftermath

On March 5, 1770, the day of the Massacre, the Townshend Acts had been repealed, except for a duty on tea. This duty was kept to remind the colonists that Parliament was supreme and had the right to govern the colonies.

Now that the chief cause for colonial unrest had been removed and the British troops had departed from the center of the city, Boston became less riotous. The nonimportation agreement had been bad for business, and besides that, many of the merchants had been dismayed by the mobs and the lawlessness. As men of property, they were a little alarmed by the more radical of the colonial agitators. Quietly they withdrew their support from this group, which began to depend more than ever on the allegiance of workingmen and the poorer people.

There followed three years of comparative calm in the colonies until, in 1773, the dispute over the duty on tea started the chain of events that made the American Revolution inevitable.

How important was the Boston Massacre in all the incidents that led up to the Revolution? Historians have differing answers to this question. Some say the disturbance made little difference one way or another; others think it may have played a significant part.

Certainly it was tremendously important as a piece of propaganda against the British. American patriots were well aware of this. For some years thereafter, on March 5, Boston was all but drowned

A broadside monumental inscription on the Boston Massacre, printed in 1772. (Prints Division, New York Public Library)

in a flood of laments and oratory. Such descriptions of the British troops as "gunning furies gloating on their carnage" certainly did nothing to promote a spirit of brotherly love for the soldiers. The Bostonians had come face to face with the troops, and there lingered the thought that what had happened once might well happen again. Their minds had been prepared for what eventually took place — the fight for independence.

Years later, one man who had witnessed some of the happenings of that violent night gave his opinion: "On that night the foundation of American independence was laid," wrote John Adams. "Not the battle of Lexington or Bunker Hill, not the surrender of Burgoyne or Cornwallis were more important events in American history than the battle of King Street on the 5th of March, 1770. The death of four or five persons, the most obscure and inconsiderable that could have been found upon the continent, has never yet been forgiven by any part of America."

BIBLIOGRAPHY

The following works have been helpful in the writing of this book:

Adams, John. *Legal Papers of John Adams*. 3 vols., ed. L. K. Wroth and H. B. Zobel. Cambridge, Mass.: Harvard University Press, 1965.

Braeman, John. *The Road To Independence: a Documentary History of the Causes of the American Revolution: 1763-1776*. New York: G. P. Putnam's Sons (Capricorn Books), 1963.

Kidder, Frederic. *History of the Boston Massacre, March 5, 1770, consisting of the Narrative of the Town, the Trial of the Soldiers, and a Historical Introduction Containing Unpublished Documents of John Adams and Explanatory Notes*. Albany, N.Y.: Joel Munsell, 1870.

Miller, John C. *Origins of the American Revolution*. Stanford, Calif.: Stanford University Press, 1959.

Morris, Richard. *Government and Labor in Early America*. New York: Octagon Press, 1965.

Shy, John. *Toward Lexington: the British Army in America*. Princeton, N.J.: Princeton University Press, 1965.

Van Tyne, Claude H. *The Causes of the War of Independence*. New York: Peter Smith, 1951.

INDEX